P9-DGE-811

PATCHWORK OF THE HEART
ADULT COLORING BOOK
COLOR Quilting Patterns & Scenes of Amish Life

PASSIO

Worry ends where faith begins.

—AMISH PROVERB

Turning the Pieces of Your Story Into a Work of Art

Each square of a quilt is used to create a beautiful, useful, and carefully mended final product. Some squares have intricate designs on them, others are plain and are used only to connect one part to another. When quilters begin, they know what the final image of the quilt will be. It is a long process, carefully designed and crafted to tell someone's story. In the same way God knew your life story as He pieced you together in the womb. God knows you, and He knows what you need. His Word provides assurance and direction for every situation you face, from the plain days to the elaborately designed ones. These reminders of God's goodness, combined with the beautiful artwork in this coloring book, will provide peace and hope as you let go of fear, worry, and anxiety and trust that "His mercy endures forever" (1 Chron. 16:34).

Don't miss the short quotations placed on the facing page of every design. Each one was chosen to complement the illustration while reminding you of the blessings God promises in His Word. As you color these designs, which were inspired by Amish quilt patterns and their way of life, reflect quietly on God's goodness and the many gifts He has bestowed upon you. When you are encouraged by God's loving-kindness, you may find that the cares and worries of life melt away, as stated in the Amish proverb.

Think back to times in your life when God's goodness and promises brought you through a hopeless situation or tough problem. Record these memories in this book or a journal. Reflecting on God's faithfulness will build your faith and remind you that He is able to meet every need that you face now or in your future. You can trust Him. And when you do, His peace, "which surpasses all understanding, will protect your hearts and minds through Christ Jesus" (Phil. 4:7).

It might interest you to know that the quotations in this book are taken from the Modern English Version of the Holy Bible. The Modern English Version (MEV) is the most modern translation produced in the King James tradition within the last thirty years. This formal equivalence translation maintains the beauty of the past yet provides fresh clarity for a new generation of Bible readers. If you would like more information on the MEV, please visit www.mevbible.com.

We hope you find this coloring book to be both beautiful and inspirational. And as you color, remember that the best artistic endeavors have no rules. Unleash your creativity as you experiment with colors, textures, and mediums. Freedom of self-expression will help release wellness, balance, mindfulness, and inner peace into your life, allowing you to enjoy the process as well as the finished product. When you're finished, you can frame your favorite creations for displaying or gift giving. Then post your artwork on Facebook, Twitter, or Instagram with the hashtag #FAITHINCOLOR.

Every good gift and every perfect gift is from above

and comes down from the Father of lights, with

whom is no change or shadow of turning.

—JAMES 1:17, MEV

The LORD your God will make you prosper in every work of your hand, in the offspring of your body, and in the offspring of your livestock, and in the produce of your land, for good. For the LORD will once again rejoice over you for good, just as He rejoiced over your fathers.

—DEUTERONOMY 30:9, MEV

We know that all things work together for good to those who love God, to those who are called according to His purpose.

—*Romans 8:28*, MEV

So now abide faith, hope, and love, these three.

But the greatest of these is love.

—1 CORINTHIANS 13:13, MEV

*For the L*ORD* gives wisdom; out of His mouth*

come knowledge and understanding.

*—P*ROVERBS *2:6,* MEV

Oh, give thanks to the L<small>ORD</small>, for He is good;

for His mercy endures forever.

—1 C<small>HRONICLES</small> 16:34, <small>MEV</small>

That Christ may dwell in your hearts through faith; that you, being rooted and grounded in love, may be able to comprehend with all saints what is the breadth and length and depth and height, and to know the love of Christ which surpasses knowledge; that you may be filled with all the fullness of God.

—EPHESIANS 3:17–19, MEV

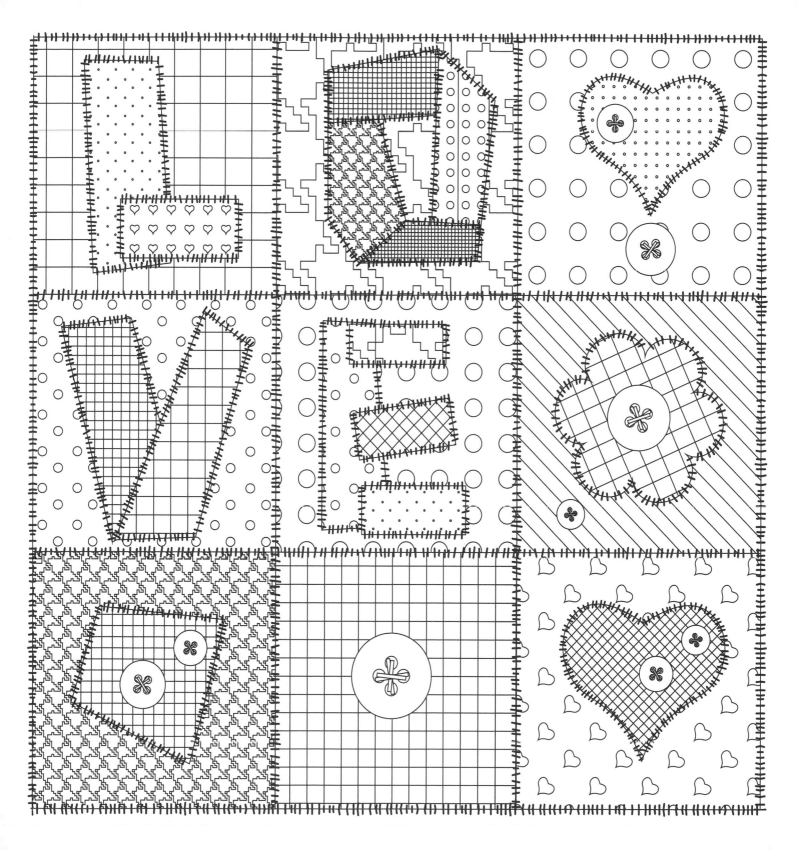

You, Lord G{\tiny OD}, have spoken, and with Your blessing,

the house of Your servant will be blessed forever.

—*2 S{\tiny AMUEL} 7:29,* {\tiny MEV}

Continue the yarn to create a frame around the scripture.

Do not let mercy and truth forsake you; bind them around your neck, write them on the tablet of your heart, so you will find favor and good understanding in the sight of God and man.

—PROVERBS 3:3–4, MEV

Our light affliction, which lasts but for a moment, works

for us a far more exceeding and eternal weight of glory,

while we do not look at the things which are seen, but at the

things which are not seen. For the things which are seen are

temporal, but the things which are not seen are eternal.

—2 CORINTHIANS 4:17–18, MEV

Do not be wise in your own eyes; fear the

LORD and depart from evil. It will be health

to your body, and strength to your bones.

—PROVERBS 3:7–8, MEV

Blessed be the LORD who has given rest to His people Israel according to all that He promised. Not one word of His promises which He gave by the hand of Moses His servant has failed.

—*1 KINGS 8:56,* MEV

Therefore be imitators of God as beloved children.

Walk in love, as Christ loved us and gave Himself for us

as a fragrant offering and a sacrifice to God.

—*EPHESIANS 5:1–2, MEV*

Walk in love, as Christ loved us and gave Himself for us as a fragrant offering and a sacrifice to God.

Ephesians 5:2

I will make all My goodness pass before you, and I will proclaim

the name of the Lᴏʀᴅ before you. I will be gracious to whom I will

be gracious and will show mercy on whom I will show mercy.

—*Exodus 33:19,* ᴍᴇᴠ

The Lord is good, a stronghold in the day of distress;

and He knows those who take refuge in Him.

—Nahum 1:7, mev

For everything created by God is good, and not to be refused if it is received with thanksgiving, for it is sanctified by the word of God and prayer.

—*1 Timothy 4:4–5*, MEV

For everything created by God is good...

1 Timothy 4:4

You gave Your good Spirit to instruct them, did not

withhold Your manna from their mouth, and

gave them water for their thirst.

—*NEHEMIAH 9:20, MEV*

Men of Israel, hear these words: Jesus of Nazareth was a man attested

to you by God with powerful works and wonders and signs, which

God did through Him in your midst, as you yourselves know. You have

taken Him, who was handed over to you by the ordained counsel and

foreknowledge of God, and by lawless hands have crucified and killed

Him, whom God raised up by loosening the pull of death, because it

was not possible that He should be held by it.

—ACTS 2:22–24, MEV

Be anxious for nothing, but in everything, by prayer and supplication

with gratitude, make your requests known to God.

—PHILIPPIANS 4:6, MEV

Now He who supplies seed to the sower and supplies

bread for your food will also multiply your seed sown

and increase the fruits of your righteousness.

—2 Corinthians 9:10, MEV

Know therefore that the L<small>ORD</small> *your God, He is God, the faithful*

God, who keeps covenant and mercy with them who love Him

and keep His commandments to a thousand generations.

—D<small>EUTERONOMY</small> 7:9, <small>MEV</small>

Therefore, I say to you, take no thought about your life, what you will eat, or what you will drink, nor about your body, what you will put on. Is not life more than food and the body than clothing? Look at the birds of the air, for they do not sow, nor do they reap, nor gather into barns. Yet your heavenly Father feeds them. Are you not much better than they?

—MATTHEW 6:25–26, MEV

Do not fear, for I am with you; do not be dismayed, for I am your God. I will strengthen you, I will help you, yes, I will uphold you with My righteous right hand.

—I*SAIAH* 41:10, MEV

He who handles a matter wisely will find good,

and whoever trusts in the LORD, happy is he.

—PROVERBS 16:20, MEV

My soul magnifies the Lord, and my spirit rejoices in God my Savior.

—LUKE 1:46–47, MEV

*The spirit of man is the candle of the L*ORD*,*

searching all the inward parts of the heart.

—PROVERBS *20:27,* MEV

Blessed is the man who hears me, watching daily at my gates, waiting at the posts of my doors. For whoever finds me finds life, and will obtain favor of the Lord.

—Proverbs 8:34–35, MEV

Now may the God of hope fill you with all joy and

peace in believing, so that you may abound in

hope, through the power of the Holy Spirit.

—Romans 15:13, MEV

Love suffers long and is kind; love envies not; love flaunts not itself and is not puffed up, does not behave itself improperly, seeks not its own, is not easily provoked, thinks no evil; rejoices not in iniquity, but rejoices in the truth; bears all things, believes all things, hopes all things, and endures all things.

—1 Corinthians 13:4–7, mev

For the L<small>ORD</small> your God is bringing you into a good land, a land of brooks of water, of fountains and springs that flow out of valleys and hills.

—D<small>EUTERONOMY</small> 8:7, <small>MEV</small>

In Him we have redemption through His blood and the forgiveness of sins according to the riches of His grace, which He lavished on us in all wisdom and insight, making known to us the mystery of His will, according to His good pleasure, which He purposed in Himself, as a plan for the fullness of time, to unite all things in Christ, which are in heaven and on earth.

—*Ephesians 1:7–10, MEV*

Pray in the Spirit always with all kinds of prayer and supplication. To that end be alert with all perseverance and supplication for all the saints.

—EPHESIANS 6:18, MEV

Beloved, let us love one another, for love is of God, and everyone who loves is born of God and knows God. Anyone who does not love does not know God, for God is love.

—1 John 4:7–8 <small>MEV</small>

He will love you and bless you and multiply you.

He will also bless the fruit of your womb and the fruit of

your land, your grain, and your wine, and your oil, the

increase of your herd and the young of your flock, in the

land which He swore to your fathers to give you.

—Deuteronomy 7:13, mev

He will love you and bless you and multiply you... The fruit of your land, grain, and wine

Deuteronomy 7:13

And I will make an everlasting covenant with them that I will not turn away from them, to do them good. But I will put My fear in their hearts so that they shall not depart from Me. Indeed, I will rejoice over them to do them good, and I will plant them in this land assuredly with My whole heart and with My whole soul.

—Jeremiah 32:40–41, mev

I told them that the hand of my God had been good to

me and also about the king's words that he had spoken

to me. And they said, "Let us rise up and build!" So they

strengthened their hands for the good work.

—NEHEMIAH 2:18, MEV

I am the vine, you are the branches. He who remains in Me,

and I in him, bears much fruit.

—John 15:5, MEV

They were joyful and good of heart because of what the

Lord had done for David, Solomon, and His people Israel.

—2 Chronicles 7:10, MEV

Pleasant words are as a honeycomb,

sweet to the soul and health to the bones.

—*Proverbs 16:24,* MEV

Do not be grieved, for the joy of the LORD is your strength.

—*NEHEMIAH 8:10, MEV*

Therefore, whether you eat, or drink, or whatever

you do, do it all to the glory of God.

—1 CORINTHIANS 10:31, MEV

Therefore, whether you eat, or drink...

...do it all to the glory of God.

1 Corinthians 10:31

For as the earth brings forth her buds, and as the garden causes the things that are sown in it to spring forth, so the Lord God will cause righteousness and praise to spring forth before all the nations.

—Isaiah 61:11, MEV

Create your own floral design inside the center square on the next page.

He said to him, "Well done, good servant!

Because you have been faithful in very

little, take authority over ten cities."

—LUKE 19:17, MEV

We give thanks to God always for you all,

mentioning you in our prayers, remembering

without ceasing your work of faith, labor of love,

and patient hope in our Lord Jesus Christ in the

sight of God and our Father.

—1 Thessalonians 1:2–3, MEV

Remember, I am with you always, even to the end of the age.

—MATTHEW 28:20, MEV

Follow the pattern of sound teaching which you have heard from me in the faith and love that is in Christ Jesus.

—*2 Timothy 1:13,* MEV

Design Director: Justin Evans
Cover Design: Justin Evans
Interior Design: Justin Evans, Lisa Rae McClure, Vincent Pirozzi

Illustrations: Getty Images / Depositphotos

International Standard Book Number: 978-1-62998-777-4

First edition

16 17 18 19 20 — 987654321

Printed in the United States of America